Helen Ivory

Maps of the Abandoned City

Dear Rafe
With warmest
wishes,

SV Helen x

SurVision Books

Feb 2019

First published in 2019 by
SurVision Books
Dublin, Ireland
www.survisionmagazine.com

Copyright © Helen Ivory, 2019

Cover image © Helen Ivory, 2019

Design © SurVision Books, 2019

ISBN: 978-1-912963-04-1

Get your moustaches together, you're going on a journey.

—Serbian proverb

CONTENTS

In a Time Before Maps	5
The Cartographer Invents Herself	6
Streets of the Abandoned City	7
the forest outside the city	8
The Cartographer Takes a Day Off	9
The Story of the City	10
The Square of the Clockmaker	11
The Hungry Mirrors	12
Nights in the Abandoned City	13
The Photograph Albums of the Abandoned City	14
The Tales	15
snapshots of the city	16
Zoo of the Abandoned City	18
Luncheon in the Abandoned City	19
The Art Gallery	20
Sister	21
Cathedral of The Abandoned City	22
The Cats and the Mice	23
Oui Ja	24
The Birds	25
Dusk	26
Sleep	27
Music of the Abandoned City	28
Outside the City Walls	29
The Cartographer Unmakes	30

In a Time Before Maps

Long ago when the city was an infant
it lay on its back on a big white sheet
transfixed by the tiny articulations
of its own small hands.

Constellations of eyes beheld from the sky –
the city grew vivid, grew hearty,
grew schools and grew graveyards
and when these were replete, it grew more.

Straw begat sticks, then sticks begat brick
so the wolf packed its bags
and decamped to the forest.
The city sprouted a gate and then locked it.

Even the city became lost in those days –
took itself for a wander inside its own head
and simply vanished. Something had to be done.
The Cartographer stepped from a fold in the sky.

The Cartographer Invents Herself

Thunder loped across the sky's wilderness
and clouds stumbled around
then fixed upon an almost-shape.

The Cartographer feels her hands
for the first time, lifts them to her face
and expertly moulds her own eyes.

She draws the roads that will carry her blood
and the pathways to order her ribcage
then hollows out a playground for her breath.

Streets of the Abandoned City

The Street of the Candlemaker runs slant to the river
where time is detained in slight tallow bodies,
moored up in ragboats awaiting the tide.

The Street of the Illusionist was never there,
or so it would have you believe;
an empty black bag in a vat full of pitch.

The Street of the Graveyard is lined with books,
with symbols and scorings no one can decipher
and carvings of cherubs too weighty to fly.

The Street of the Birds is a vault of locked cages,
each inhabitant rendered to feather and bone.
Wind blusters through keyholes to parody song.

The Street of the Kings wears a crown of eye teeth
plucked from the jaws of anonymous dogs.
The Street of the Dogs was scratched from the map.

the forest outside the city

is bedlam with birdsong
each flashy morning

gravid with wolfsong
all the long nights

is pathless as a cauldron
hung over a pyre

don't unbolt the gates
warned the mournful breeze

keep away from the shadows
mouthed the shadows

The Cartographer Takes a Day Off

It was Sunday after all, and the last cul-de-sac
had been crossed and then dotted.
She put the lid on her ink and went walking.
Not a soul was abroad in those familiar streets,
the city gate was unarmed and wide open.

Outside the walls she stretched her legs
and was presently eye to eye with the treetops.
The coast lay but a breath away
and the sea, pleased as a puppy, greeted her,
rolled to show its belly by degrees.

An age ago, she had tried to map the sea
but they had come to an understanding.
She wasn't that kind of a map-maker
and the sea wasn't that kind of sea.
They met at the rag of shore from time to time.

It was the variety of summer day you'd find in books
but this story is still waiting for a pen to write it down.
Instead we'll see some images –
a man digs feverishly into the washed-out sand,
a single magpie draws a line through the sun.

The Story of the City

It all began a long time ago as stories are wont to do. It began with wolves, but wolves were too fierce, so they were written out of the story. The story really begins when some of the cast-out wolves turned their coats inside-out and called themselves dogs. Their paws grew soft, so people took pity and invited them into their homes. Some of the people envied the dogs and asked that their fur be groomed too. And with their fur so sleek, they asked that others manage their claws, and with their claws to tidy and clean, they asked that their food be bought to them on golden trays. Soon they wore cloaks to protect their sleek fur and went about the city as if they owned it. They were so convinced, the rest of the people believed it too. And it was deemed right that their golden trays be piled high, while others' bowls were left empty save a few grains now and then.

One day, a wolf stood on a hill and looked down on the city. She howled to her children to come join her in the world. The dogs went first and then people, one by one, until only a handful of those ones in cloaks were left. They held their golden trays up to the sky, begging for sweetmeats, but with no hands left to feed them; they died.

The Square of the Clockmaker

When the last train left,
the tunnel rolled the train track
back into its mouth and slept.

Clocks unhitched themselves
from the made-up world of timetables
and opened wide their arms.

And in the square of the clockmaker
a century of clocks
turned their faces to the sun.

The Hungry Mirrors

The mirrors of the abandoned city
are hungry as hungry can be.
At least the lakes have a bellyful of sky.
At least the ponds are heavy with livestock.

These days, it's drawn blinds,
empty changing rooms
and the chirruping crickets
they have no ears for.

Once, a spider hauled itself
down by a thread
and they gorged on it frantically,
like someone lost in the desert.

Ah, those starveling servants of vanity,
we must pity them in their lean days –
when all eternity is an empty great coat
in the maw of an unlit corridor.

Nights in the Abandoned City

Dark comes home to the abandoned city
and heaves off its boots by the fire.
It is astonishing how weary the dark is from its work,
its commute through choking towns and encampments.

It talks to the flames of the things it has seen
of the stilled hearts it has held
between finger and thumb.
It unburdens itself of all human sorrow.

And the fire, pretending for now
it is a hearth at the centre of a church house,
listens like a priest and bites its own tongue,
imbues the parlour with cloying incense.

In the shadowplay, the dark is a plague doctor's mask,
a bone-saw, a gathering of spat-out teeth.
Soon, fire will describe a still life of eyeglasses:
their tiny infinities – all their dashed lenses.

The Photograph Albums of the Abandoned City

The families have arranged themselves,
have organised dogs and tables.

Some have baked cakes,
others hold fish or babies as offerings.

A man has made a pact with gravity
and floats over a staircase, umbrella in hand.

Light has leeched into the body
of the camera

so the bride wears a black dress,
a garland of shadows.

The Tales

*

The maid stood at the edge of the city and opened the cage of her chest. Her heart preened its wings of arterial blood and then flew. Up it went, high, high as the cathedral spire. She returned to the palace and made beds, tight as drums.

*

One morning, when the cloak-maker had finished a long night of stitching, his fingers aching, the fabric spotted with his own blood, he sat in the stillness and observed his labours. Even the sun was not stout enough to penetrate the deep valleys of the cloak.

*

What use is a head? thought the gardener as he scythed off his own and those of his groundsmen. The heads rolled into the palace's ha-ha. Bees were occupied like any other day. A mole mined a path under the neat rolled lawn.

snapshots of the city

*

three cups
their orbital saucers
a rorschach of milk froth.
a yellow dog
tied to the railings.

*

an apple tree
blighted by frogeye.
rain in conversation
with a chair
belly-up in the park.

*

heads, all of them
stacked in a box
sewn together
by cellar spiders,
mouth to ear.

*
a fox moth
panhandles
what's left of the light.
a ragged tent
pitched in a yard.

*

two forks
locked together
at the edge of a road.
the geography of landfill,
the surrendering to dust.

Zoo of the Abandoned City

With the biddable and winsome gone
the zoo is a graver place of sharp eyes and fangs.
The small and portable are piqued
they've been deserted here
and funnel spiders have long memories.

Cages were left unlatched
(the keepers were not beasts after all)
so everyone is free to come and go
at their own leisure and, well, peril.
Caimans have made Monkey Walk a no-go zone.

Inmates are balanced on their nerves
like high-wire acts within a wide cupola;
are scrappily made effigies of themselves
held out to the rain that leans in
before continuing its rounds.

Luncheon in the Abandoned City

There have been no hands
to wind clocks for months now
thus, restaurants rely on instinct
and the shadows on pavements
to signal when to prepare for service.

Only salt and pulses remain
so, ladles spend the morning
meting them out in melancholy portions
onto row upon row
of poker-faced plates.

At noon, cutlery goes through the motions –
a mechanical dance of luncheon
gnashing salt into powder
agitating the pulses
till the gong shudders
            and they all fall down.

The Art Gallery

clears its throat and holds forth
to the symposium's audience
of one hundred and twenty stacking chairs,
a water cooler with seven plastic cups, and a broom.

Is it a given then, that these Old Masters
are shorn of their aesthetic and their monetary value
when there are no human eyes to feast here?
it asserts, getting into its stride.

The water-cooler gurgles crankily in response,
the broom agitates the dust
while the faces on the walls look
as they have looked for tongue-tied centuries.

20

Sister

The moon is weary of the City's halogens
and neon flamingos;
its spangling vauntings of plastic glamour.

If the moon could anthropomorphicise itself
she would be a sister in a hospital drama
with judgemental eyebrows and sanitized hands.

She would stand at the edge of the ward
one eye on the casino
the other on the pelican crossing.

She would summon the sea
to this landlocked place
and tuck it in snug with hospital corners.

Cathedral of The Abandoned City

A thrush flew at a rose window
broke its neck and lay dead in the grass
so the imprint of a dusty angel
watches over the deserted pews.

An avenue of tombstones –
a whole family – forms the path
to a dark pond, thick with lilies
and a miracle of pond skaters.

Each night the congregation appears
like an unfixed Calotype
to an audience of mice
hearts skipping in their tiny chests.

The Cats and the Mice

When all had been absent of human noise
for three turns of the moon,
the cats and the mice came to an understanding.

Mice would reign in the cheese shop
while cats would claim sovereignty
of the fishmongers.

There will be no Tom-and-Jerry-style absurdities.
No sticks of dynamite applied
to the rolled-out tongues of sleeping cats

and no mouse need squander a bead of sweat
on hefting irons to rooves
in the hope a cat would mosey by.

Thus, began a golden age, which like each golden age
will soon prove itself to be composite metal
with gilding shown greenish as it rubs away.

A mouse in a cloak stands on the last cheese wheel.
A cat in a cloak holds the last sole aloft.
It's the cats' fault! said the mouse. *Greedy mice!* said the cat.

Hence, the Battle of the Grocery Shop began.
The mouse shouting orders with a mouth full of brie.
The cat screaming *attack!* spitting sole at the ranks.

Oui Ja

On the Street of the Clairvoyants
an unmanned Oui Ja board
is rapidly shifting a sherry glass.

A long-dead lion-tamer
is anxious to have the last word
in a long-standing feud with the ringmaster.

A stuttering pharmacist
spells out the periodic table,
glass faltering over the O of oxygen.

Moreover, Alice needs to speak to Lawrence,
but there is nobody there
to take the call.

She frantically moves the glass to *yes*
yes yes and then, *I do* –
the door rattling against its jamb.

The Birds

During the final days of those final days
the city gate was propped open for stragglers
dragging their suitcases through windy streets –
civilization's chip-wrappers jamming their wheels.

And then a rustling of a million feathers
as all the sky's birds
put their shoulder to the gate
and closed it, as if closing a tomb.

A whirlwind of litter baffled about the city –
until a crow with one blue eye
rose, gave an ushering caw,
and thence the assembly swooped.

For six days and six nights they worked
with unstinting precision
to garner each cast-off wrapping, each scuttling drink can,
each motley fragment of plastic.

On the seventh day, urged on by the crow,
they conjured a structure from this debris,
a structure surpassing any manmade fabrication.
A nest, a glorious nest reaching out to the high heavens!

Dusk

At the amusement arcade
an out-of-date fortune teller
keeps pedalling her cards
inside her electric booth.

Nobody thought to unplug her
so the future is pushed forward
on lavender cards
with a fleur-de-lis motif.

A stranger will call with tidings from afar.
Beware the season's turn!
One of the light bulbs is out
casting her left side in shadow.

Sleep

The city is old.
It pulls furs about itself,
hunkers down and draws archetypes
on the insides of its eyelids with chalk:

a staircase stopping to consider
if it is going up or down,
a bed empty as a ploughed field,
a discarded sheet miming snow.

These days there is nothing
you can say to bestir the city.
No seraphim or hooded minstrel
to pour music through its underground trains.

Music of the Abandoned City

In the Street of Sunk Melodies
the sky is a scrim
of leaves on black water.

A monkey huddles on a riverboat
dismantling the barrel organ
pressed to its belly

removing the pins
with long-nosed pliers
and casting them overboard.

The river runs its fingers over the notes
as it catches them
and swells to its banks with a babel.

Outside the City Walls

The Beast shakes itself down,
looses the mizzle from its pelt.
The rainfall had kept it awake
through the centuries
and it felt satisfying at last
to confront it.

The Beast had pulled
the clouds apart with its jaws,
raised its hackles
and howled at the thunder
like a man affecting the cries of a wolf.
It rolls in straw to dry itself.

There really was nothing out there
but meteorological conditions.
The Beast should have listened
to its mother on that score.
It looks along its own sullen shadow
and wonders if that is a fiction too.

The Cartographer Unmakes

It's snow that gives her the idea,
bleaching parks of desire lines
and blotting out coffin paths.
With a white paintbrush
she makes a halo of the ring road
and cancels out the tower blocks and castle.

And when there is no one left
to remember the City,
when all has turned to fireside yarns and myth,
a traveller will open out
some spotless pages of the map
and imagine lady fortune shines on him.

More poetry published by SurVision Books

Noelle Kocot. *Humanity*
(New Poetics: USA)
ISBN 978-1-9995903-0-7

Ciaran O'Driscoll. *The Speaking Trees*
(New Poetics: Ireland)
ISBN 978-1-9995903-1-4

Elin O'Hara Slavick. *Cameramouth*
(New Poetics: USA)
ISBN 978-1-9995903-4-5

Anatoly Kudryavitsky. *Stowaway*
(New Poetics: Ireland)
ISBN 978-1-9995903-2-1

George Kalamaras. *That Moment of Wept*
ISBN 978-1-9995903-7-6

Christopher Prewitt. *Paradise Hammer*
(Winner of James Tate Poetry Prize 2018)
ISBN 978-1-9995903-9-0

Anton Yakovlev. *Chronos Dines Alone*
(Winner of James Tate Poetry Prize 2018)
ISBN 978-1-912963-01-0

Bob Lucky. *Conversation Starters in the Language No One Speaks*
(Winner of James Tate Poetry Prize 2018)
ISBN 978-1-912963-00-3

Mikko Harvey & Jake Bauer. *Idaho Falls*
(Winner of James Tate Poetry Prize 2018)
ISBN 978-1-912963-02-7

Maria Grazia Calandrone. *Fossils*
Translated from Italian
(New Poetics: Italy)
ISBN 978-1-9995903-6-9

Sergey Biryukov. *Transformations*
Translated from Russian
(New Poetics: Russia)
ISBN 978-1-9995903-5-2

Anton G. Leitner. *Selected Poems 1981–2015*
Translated from German
ISBN 978-1-9995903-8-3

Our books are available to order via
http://survisionmagazine.com/books.htm